C000084492

Table of Contents

Presentation

Drop 10 pounds in one week and never gain it back. You can do it if you follow the Dukan Diet's rules, claims French general practitioner and nutritionist Pierre Dukan, who made the eating routine in 2000.

Presentation

Drop 10 pounds in one week and never gain it back. You can do it if you follow the Dukan Diet's rules, claims French general practitioner and nutritionist Pierre Dukan, who made the eating regimen in 2000.

Lean protein, oat wheat, water, and a daily 20-minute walk are at the heart of the plan. The hypothesis is that limiting carbohydrates forces your body to consume fat.

Basically, you can eat limitless amounts of food, as long as they're on the approved foods list, which incorporates very few carbs, if any.

Lean protein, oat wheat, water, and a daily 20-minute walk are at the heart of the plan. The hypothesis is that limiting carbohydrates forces your body to consume fat.

Basically, you can eat limitless amounts of food, as long as they're on the approved foods list, which incorporates very few carbs, if any.

What is the Dukan Diet?

The Dukan Diet is a high-protein, low-carb weight loss diet that is split into four phases.

It was created by Dr. Pierre Dukan, a French general practitioner who specializes in weight management.

Dr. Dukan created the diet in the 1970s, inspired by an obese patient who said he could give up eating any food in order to lose weight, with the exception of meat.

After seeing many of his patients experience impressive weight loss results on his diet, Dr. Dukan published The Dukan Diet in 2000.

The book was eventually released in 32 countries and became a major bestseller. It reportedly helped people achieve rapid, easy weight loss without hunger.

The Dukan Diet shares some features of the high-protein, low-carb Stillman Diet, along with the Atkins Diet.

Summary

The Dukan Diet is a high-protein, low-carb weight loss diet that is claimed to produce rapid weight loss without hunger.

How does it work?

The Dukan Diet starts by calculating your goal weight — called your "true" weight — based on your age, weight loss history, and other factors.

How long you stay in each phase depends on how much weight you need to lose to reach your "true" weight.

These are the four phases of the Dukan diet:

- Attack Phase (1–7 days): You start the diet by eating unlimited lean protein plus 1.5 tablespoons of oat bran per day.

- Cruise Phase (1–12 months): Alternate lean protein one day with lean protein and non-starchy veggies the next, plus 2 tablespoons of oat bran every day.

- Consolidation Phase (5 days for every pound lost in phases 1 and 2): Unlimited lean protein and veggies, some carbs and fats, one day of lean protein weekly, 2.5 tablespoons of oat bran daily.

- Stabilization Phase (indefinite): Follow the Consolidation Phase guidelines but loosen the rules as long as your weight remains stable. Oat bran is increased to 3 tablespoons per day.

Foods to include and avoid

Each phase of the Dukan Diet has its own dietary pattern. Here's what you're allowed to eat during each.

Attack Phase

The Attack Phase is primarily based on high-protein foods, plus a few extras that provide minimal calories:

- Lean beef, veal, venison, bison, and other game
- Lean pork
- Poultry without skin
- Liver, kidney, and tongue

- Fish and shellfish (all types)
- Eggs
- Non-fat dairy products (restricted to 32 ounces or 1 kg per day), such as milk, yogurt, cottage cheese, and ricotta
- Tofu and tempeh
- Seitan, a meat substitute made from wheat gluten
- At least 6.3 cups (1.5 liters) of water per day (mandatory)
- 1.5 tablespoons (9 grams) of oat bran daily (mandatory)
- Unlimited artificial sweeteners, shirataki noodles, and diet gelatin
- Small amounts of lemon juice and pickles
- 1 teaspoon (5 ml) of oil daily for greasing pans

Cruise Phase

This phase alternates between two days.

On day one, dieters are restricted to foods from the Attack Phase. On day two, they're allowed Attack Phase foods plus the following vegetables:

Spinach, kale, lettuce, and other leafy greens

Broccoli, cauliflower, cabbage, and Brussels sprouts

- o Bell peppers
- o Asparagus
- o Artichokes
- o Eggplant
- o Cucumbers
- o Celery

- Tomatoes
- Mushrooms
- Green beans
- Onions, leeks, and shallots
- Spaghetti squash
- Pumpkin
- Turnips
- 1 serving of carrots or beets daily
- 2 tablespoons (12 grams) of oat bran daily (mandatory)

No other vegetables or fruits are permitted. Other than 1 teaspoon (5 ml) of oil in salad dressing or for greasing pans, no fat should be added.

Consolidation Phase

During this phase, dieters are encouraged to mix and match any of the foods from the Attack and Cruise Phases, along with the following:

- Fruit: One serving of fruit per day, such as 1 cup (100 grams) of berries or chopped melon; one medium apple, orange, pear, peach, or nectarine; or two kiwis, plums, or apricots.
- Bread: Two slices of whole-grain bread per day, with a small amount of reduced-fat butter or spread.
- Cheese: One serving of cheese (1.5 ounces or 40 grams) per day.
- Starches: 1–2 servings of starches per week, such as 8 ounces (225 grams) of pasta and

other grains, corn, beans, legumes, rice, or
potatoes.

- Meat: Roast lamb, pork or ham 1–2 times
  per week.
- Celebration meals: Two "celebration meals"
  per week, including one appetizer, one main
  dish, one dessert and one glass of wine.
- Protein meal: One "pure proteins" day per
  week, where only foods from the Attack
  Phase are allowed.
- Oat bran: 2.5 tablespoons (15 grams) of oat
  bran daily (mandatory).

Stabilization Phase

The Stabilization Phase is the final phase of the
Dukan diet. It is all about maintaining the
improvements achieved during the earlier phases.

No foods are strictly off-limits, but there are a few principles to follow:

- Use the Consolidation Phase as a basic framework for planning meals.
- Continue having one "pure proteins" meal day every week.
- Never take the elevator or escalator when you can take the stairs.
- Oat bran is your friend. Take 3 tablespoons (17.5 grams) every day.

Summary

The Dukan Diet allows protein-rich foods in the first phase and protein with vegetables in the second. It adds limited portions of carbs and fats in the third phase, with looser guidelines in the final phase.

Sample meal plans

Here are sample meal plans for the first three phases of the Dukan Diet:

Attack Phase

❖ Breakfast

1. Non-fat cottage cheese with 1.5 tablespoons (9 grams) of oat bran, cinnamon and sugar substitute
2. Coffee or tea with nonfat milk and sugar substitute

3. Water

Lunch

- ✓ Roast chicken
- ✓ Shirataki noodles cooked in bouillon
- ✓ Diet gelatin
- ✓ Iced tea

Dinner

- ✓ Lean steak and shrimp
- ✓ Diet gelatin
- ✓ Decaf coffee or tea with nonfat milk and sugar substitute
- ✓ Water

Cruise Phase

Breakfast

- ➤ Three scrambled eggs
- ➤ Sliced tomatoes
- ➤ Coffee with nonfat milk and sugar substitute
- ➤ Water

Lunch

- ➤ Grilled chicken on mixed greens with low-fat vinaigrette
- ➤ Greek yogurt, 2 tablespoons (12 grams) of oat bran and sugar substitute

- Iced tea

Dinner

- Baked salmon fillet
- Steamed broccoli and cauliflower
- Diet gelatin
- Decaf coffee with nonfat milk and sugar substitute
- Water

Consolidation Phase

Breakfast

- Omelet made with three eggs, 1.5 ounces (40 grams) of cheese and spinach
- Coffee with nonfat milk and sugar substitute
- Water

Lunch

- Turkey sandwich on two slices of whole-wheat bread
- 1/2 cup (81 grams) of cottage cheese with 2 tablespoons (12 grams) of oat bran, cinnamon and sugar substitute
- Iced tea

Dinner

- Roast pork

- Grilled zucchini
- 1 medium apple
- Decaf coffee with nonfat milk and sugar substitute
- Water

Summary

Meals on the Dukan Diet include plenty of meat, vegetables, oat bran, tea, and coffee.

Recipes for Dukan Diet

Cinnamon & Caramel Cheesecake

I just love any kind of cheesecake. It is so easy to prepare and you just need some usual ingredients, not expensive at all. I like to flavour my cheesecake each time and when I want to spoil myself I put a fruit sauce on top! So perfect!

Ingredients:

-500 g Philadelphia cheese, or other lox-fat soft cheese

- 150 g greek yogurt or low fat soured cream

- 2 eggs

- 4-5 tbsp sweetener

-2 tbsp corn starch (only from Cruise phase)

- 1 tsp caramel essence/sauce (sugar free)

- 1 tsp cinnamon

How to prepare:

1. Preheat the oven to 180oC/350oF/Gas 4

2. Mix cheese with yogurt (or sour cream), eggs, sweetener and corn starch.

3. Homogenized composition really well then add the caramel essence and cinnamon.

4. Put the composition in a tray and bake it in the oven for about 40-45 minutes.

5. Let the cheesecake cool, then put in the fridge for 3 hours or overnight.

Enjoy my dukan recipe!

Raspberry Cheesecake

I think I told you that cheesecake is one of my favorite desserts. This time I tried the raspberry cheesecake and this recipe it is suitable for those who are in consolidation or Dukan diet Dukan Express.

It has a good flavor and a fine texture. Just perfect!

Ingredients for the sponge (tray with 18-20 cm diameter):

-2 egg whites

- 1 egg yolk

- 1 tsp konjac flour (or 1 tbsp corn starch)

- 2 tbsp oat bran

- 2 tbsp sweetener

- vanilla flavouring

Cheese-layer ingredients:

-500 fat free cream cheese (ricotta, Philadelphia))

- 150g fat free greek yogurt

- 1 egg

- 2 tbsp cornstarch

- 4 lg sweetener

- vanilla flavouring

- 1 cup raspberries

Topping Ingredients:

-1 Cup raspberries

Jelly Ingredients:

- 100 ml sugar free raspberry syrup

- 3 gelatin leaves (or 1 tsp)

How to prepare:

Preheat the oven to 180oC/350oF/Gas 4.

1. Whisk the egg whites with a pinch of salt until very firm, then add the yolk and the konjac flour and keep mixing for 2-3 minutes.

2. Add the sweetener, the bran and vanilla essence and pour the mixture in the tray

3. Bake 12 to 15 minutes at 180 degrees.

4. In a separate bowl combine all the ingredients for the cheese layer, except the raspberries. Add the raspberries and mix gently not to break them.

5. Pour the cheese over the sponge and put the try back in the oven for 50-60 minutes. When done, leave it to cool.

6. It is time for the raspberry jelly. Soak gelatine leaves in cold water. Dissolve the hydrated gelatine leaves in the preheated raspberries syrup.

7. When the cheesecake is cold enough put some raspberries on top and then pour the jelly over (do not take the cheesecake off the tray).

8. Place in the refrigerator for at least 2 hour before eating. Eat cold!

Enjoy my dukan recipe!

Pain Doux (French Sweet Bread)

I totally love this sweet bread! You can use it to make different cakes with cream cheese or some pudding.

You can also take off the sweetener and replace it with salt and you will have a fluffy bread!

Ingredients:

-4 eggs

- 4 tbsp oat bran

- 6 tbsp skimmed milk powder

- 4-5 tbsp powdered sweetener

- 1 tsp vanilla essence

- 1 tbsp baking powder

- few strands of saffron

How to prepare:

1. Preheat the oven to 180oC/350oF/Gas 4.

2. Separate egg whites and whisk the egg whites with a pinch of salt until very firm.

3. Add the egg yolks and sweetener and mixing 1-2 minutes.

4. Replace mixer with a spoon and add the oat bran and skimmed milk powder, then mix slowly in composition from top to bottom.

5. Add the vanilla, baking powder and saffron.

6. Using a spoon pour the mixture into silicone reusable baking cups or in one tray.

7. Place in the oven and bake for about 20-25 minutes. Allow to cool and eaten with pleasure.

Enjoy my dukan recipe!

Baked chicken with cherry tomatoes and peppers

Ingredients:

-4-5 boneless chicken thighs

- 2 peppers

- 6-8 cherry tomatoes

- 1-2 cloves of garlic

- 1 tbsp olive oil

-2 tsp italian herbs

- salt, pepper

- 250 ml water or chicken broth

How to prepare:

1. Preheat oven to 350 degrees F (175 degrees C)

2.Place the chicken thighs in a pan or oven dish

3. Cut the peppers into large pieces and cherry tomatoes in half and place them in / on the chicken pieces

4. Season with italian herbs, salt and pepper

5. Sprinkle with olive oil and add the water or chicken broth and.

6. Bake in the oven for 50-60 minutes until brown the chicken and the vegetables soften.

Enjoy my dukan recipe!

Baked Chicken with Vegetables

Ingredients:

-2-4 Chicken drumsticks

- 1 red pepper

- 1 onion

- 1 zucchini

- 2 cloves of garlic

-3-4 Cherry tomatoes

- 1 tbsp olive oil

- ½ tbsp sweet paprika

- ½ tbsp garlic powder

- Salt and pepper

- 1 tbsp oregano

How to prepare:

1. Preheat oven to 350 degrees F (175 degrees C).

2.Cut the vegetables into larger cubes and put them in the tray

3.Mix olive oil with sweet paprika, garlic powder, salt, pepper and oregano.

4. Brush the chicken drumsticks with this olive mix and put them over vegetables in the tray

5. Add water to the pot (about a cup)

6. Cover with aluminum foil or a lid and put into the oven

7. Cook in the oven about 40-45 minutes, then remove foil or lid and cook another 10-15 minutes

Enjoy your dukan meal!

Zucchini casserole

Ingredients:

-2 cups shredded zucchini

- 2 eggs

- 200 g fat free ricotta cheese

- fresh dill

- 1 tablespoon cornstarch

- 1 tablespoon finely chopped onion

- salt, pepper

How to prepare:

1. Preheat oven to 350 degrees F (175 degrees C).

2. In a small bowl, beat the eggs salt and pepper.

3. Add the zucchini, onion and the fresh dill; stir to coat.

4.Stir in cheese.

5.Pour into a 15-oz. baking dish coated with cooking spray.

6.Bake at 375° for 30 to 35 minutes. Let stand for 10 minutes before serving.

Enjoy my dukan recipe!

Cheese and smoked chicken casserole

Ingredients:

- 1 cup chopped smoked chicken or shredded purchased roasted chicken

- 300 g fat free ricotta cheese or other creamy cheese

- green onion

- 1 egg yolk

- salt, pepper

How to prepare:

1. Preheat oven to 350 degrees F (175 degrees C).

2.In a bowl mix the smoked chicken with ricotta cheese, egg yolk, green onion and salt and pepper.

3.Place them into a 9×13-inch baking dish and top with cheese (optional).

4.Bake at 350 degrees F (175 degrees C) for 35 to 40 minutes, or until cheese is melted and bubbly.

Enjoy my dukan recipe!

Buffalo Chicken Wings

Ingredients:

-8-10 chicken wings

- 3 tablespoons unsweetened ketchup

- 1 teaspoon chili powder

- 1 teaspoon garlic powder

- Salt and freshly ground black pepper

How to prepare:

1.Preheat the oven to 375 degrees F.

2.Rinse and pat dry the chicken wings.

3.Mix the ketchup, chili powder, garlic powder, and some salt and pepper in a medium bowl or resealable plastic bag.

4.Toss the wings in the seasoned mixture to coat well.

5. Place in the refrigerator for 30 minutes.

6. Bake the wings on baking sheet until very tender and the skin is crisp, 20-25 minutes.

Enjoy my dukan recipe!

Cheese and turkey Casserole

Ingredients:

- 300 g ground turkey

- 300 g fat free ricotta or cottage cheese

- 2 eggs

- salt, pepper

- some shredded fat free Cheddar cheese

How to prepare:

1.Preheat oven to 350 degrees F (175 degrees C).

2.In a large skillet over medium-high heat, saute the ground turkey for 5 to 10 minutes, or until browned.

2. Drain the turkey, stir in the ricotta cheese, eggs, salt and pepper.

3. Place them into a 9×13-inch baking dish and top with cheese.

4. Bake at 350 degrees F (175 degrees C) for 35 to 40 minutes, or until cheese is melted and bubbly.

Enjoy my dukan recipe!

Beef meatballs with konjac rice

Ingredients:

-1 pound ground beef (500 g)

- 1 small onion, finely chopped

-1 small garlic clove, minced

-1 large egg

- 1 green onion (only the green part)

- Spices (salt, pepper, garlic powder)

- 8 ounces konjac rice (250 g)

- 3 tablespoons finely chopped flat-leaf parsley and dill

How to prepare:

1.Preheat the oven to 180oC/350oF/Gas 4.

2.Rinse the rice with cold water and leave to drain in a sieve.

3.Mince your onion and garlic or put them in a food processor if you don't want to chop them.

4.Add all the ingredients in a large bowl and mix together (you can also mix by hand).

5. Form mixture into 1-20 meatballs and place on prepared pan.

6.Bake in centre of preheated oven until juices run clear, 18 to 20 minutes.

Enjoy your dukan meal!

Yogurt jelly with rum, vanilla and cinnamon

Ingredients:

- 300 g fat free greek yogurt

- 50 ml skimmed milk

- 3-4 tablespoon sweetener

- 1 tablespoon of vanilla

- 1/4 teaspoon of cinnamon

- few drops of rum essence

- 6 gelatine leaves

How to prepare:

Soak gelatine leaves in cold water. Bring milk to a
soft boil.

In a medium bowl combine yogurt, sweetener, vanilla and rum.

Dissolve gelatine leaves in milk and slowly pour into yogurt mixture stirring well.

Eggplant and tomatoes towers

Ingredients:

- 1 large eggplant

- 2 large tomatoes

- 0.4 lbs fat free ricotta or any other cream cheese

- fresh basil leaves

- 2 garlic cloves

- 1 tablespoon extra-virgin olive oil (optional)

- salt and freshly ground black pepper to taste

How to prepare:

Cut of the eggplant crosswise into 1" thick rounds
and season them with salt and leave them for 30

minutes on a side to let water to come out of the eggplant.

Once ready drizzle some olive oil on top of each slice and grill them on a lightly oiled grill rack for 2 -3 minutes each side.

Cut the tomatoes crosswise to 1/4" thick rounds.

Rum and goji ice cream

Ingredients:

-4 greek fat free yogurt (4×150 g)

- 100 ml skimmed milk

- 4 tablespoon powder skimmed milk

- 1 egg yolk (optional)

- 3-4 tbsp sweetener

- rum essence

- 2 tbsp goji

How to prepare:

You can do the ice cream using the ice cream
maker (machine) or the clasic way.

First put the goji in some water (room temperature) and rum essence and leave to hydrate for at least 5 minutes.

Drained the goji and mix them with the other ingredients in a bowl.

Place plastic wrap directly on cream mixture, and chill 8 to 24 hours.

Pour mixture into freezer container of a 1 1/2-qt. electric ice-cream maker, and freeze according to manufacturer's instructions. (Instructions and time may vary.)

When ice cream is softly frozen, serve immediately or place a piece of plastic wrap directly on the ice cream and place in freezer to ripen, 2 to 3 hours.

If you do not have an ice-cream maker don`t forget to take the bowl from the freezer and whip for 1 minute and back to the freezer. Repeat about 4 times.

Place in a container with a lid. Store in the freezer.

Enjoy my dukan recipe!

Sweet cheese muffins with goji berries

Ingredients :

-300 g fat free cheese

- 150 g fat free Greek yogurt

- 2 eggs

- 4 tbsp oat bran , preferably finely ground

- 2 tbsp cornstarch (not in atack fase)

- 4 tbsp powder skimmed milk

-3-4 tbsp sweetener

- vanilla flavouring

- ½ tsp dry yeast

- 3 tbsp goji berries

- rum flavouring

How to prepare

Preheat the oven to 180oC/350oF/Gas 4.

Hydrate the goji in some water and rum flavouring for about 10 minutes.

Whisk the the yogurt cheese and eggs. In another bowl, mix all the dry ingredients (oat bran, starch and powder milk). Use a large spoon to gently fold the wet ingredients into the dry – don't overmix, just lightly combine. Add sweetener, vanilla flavouring and dry yeast.

Mix and leave aside for 10-15 minutes. Add the water drained goji.

Using a spoon pour the mixture into 10-12 silicone reusable baking cups.

Chocolate cake

Ingredients:

-3 eggs

- 4 tbsp oat bran

- 6 tbsp powder skimmed milk

- sweetener to taste

- 2 tbsp fat free greek yogurt

- 1 tbsp instant espresso

- 1 tbsp fat free cocoa

- ½ tsp baking powder

- Vanilla quintessence

How to plan:

Preheat the oven at 180oC.

Separate egg whites and beat them with a pinch of salt until very firm. Mix the egg yolks with yogurt and pour it slowly over whites foam. Add all the dry fixings (wheat, milk powder, sugar, cocoa, instant coffee , baking powder, vanilla) and using a spoon slowly mix sythesis from top to bottom.

Pour the composition into a cake container and bake it in the oven 30-35 minutes. Leave to cool.

You can eat with some greek yogurt blend with sweetener and mint substance.

Enjoy my dukan formula!

Lemon Cheesecake

Ingredients for the sponge

- 2 egg

- 2 tbsp oat bran

- 3-4 tbsp sugar/sugar

- ¼ tsp bicarbonate

Cheesecake fixings

- 500 g low-fat cheddar

- 150 g fat Greek yogurt

- 2 eggs

- a large portion of a lime juice

- half lemon juice

- 1 tsp grated lemon peel or lemon quintessence if
needed

- 4-5 tbsp sweetener/sugar

How to prepare

Preheat the oven to 180oC/350oF/Gas 4

For the sponge, separate the egg whites from the yolks. Beat the whites with a spot of salt.

Mix remaining ingredients in a different bowl.Fold whites into the other composition.

Put the composition on a tray (around 22 cm diameter) and bake it in the oven for 10-12 min.

Meanwhile set up the cheese filling. In a bowl blend cheese with eggs, lime and lemon juice, lemon zing and sweetener. Homogenized creation really well then pour into pan over your baked sponge.

Bake it in the stove for around 40-45 minutes then leave it to cool before eating.

Enjoy my dukan recipe!

Zesty Firecracker Prawns

Ingredients

12 large Uncooked Prawns per person

Lemon Juice to coat

Ingredients for Spicy Firecracker Powder

1 teaspoon of Freshly Ground Black Pepper

1 teaspoon of Paprika

1/2 teaspoon of Dried Chili Flakes

1/2 teaspoon of Onion Powder

1/2 teaspoon of Oregano

1/2 teaspoon of Thyme

1/2 teaspoon of Garlic Powder

1/4 teaspoon of Cayenne Pepper

Method

Peel the prawns and de-vein, leaving the tails on if preferred.

Place six prawns on each skewer (2 skewers per person).

Make up your dry Spicy Firecracker Powder adjusting amounts up or down – the amounts given should coat about 6 skewers. If you make too much, it is quite good as a seasoning for chicken too. You can also increase or decrease the amounts of each ingredient until you get the taste and heat that you prefer. Make sure that you mix the ingredients well as you don't want all of the Chili Flakes or Cayenne Pepper in one place.

Brush with lemon juice and sprinkle the Firecracker Powder over both sides of the prawns.

Cook on a barbecue or grill or broil until prawns are cooked, turning halfway through.

Dukan Diet Attack Phase Recipe: Mexican Coriander Prawns

This is the third in a series of Prawn (Shrimp) Recipe Posts that I've put together just for "stephanielr" who was finding prawns a little bland. The Mexican influence in this recipe comes from the Coriander (Cilantro), Chilies and Lime Juice in the marinade. The only vegetables used are allowed condiments so this recipe is suitable for all phases of the Dukan Diet. You could serve on top of cottage cheese drizzled with a little lime juice accompanied by an oat bran pancake made with a few herbs and spices of your choice and cut into triangles.

Mexican Coriander Prawns

Ingredients

- 12 large uncooked Prawns per serving

- Ingredients for Marinade

- 1 bunch of Fresh Coriander (Cilantro)
- 8 medium Spring Onions (Scallions)
- 4 Cloves of Garlic
- 2 Green Chilies
- A tablespoon of Lime Juice
- 2 teaspoons of Cumin
- A pinch of Turmeric

Method

- Place all of the ingredients for the marinade in a food processor or blender and puree. You may need to water to get the correct consistency.
- Peel the prawns and de-vein leaving the tails on if desired.

- Place the marinade and prawns in a large bowl and coat the prawns well with the marinade.
- Cover the bowl with cling film and place in the refrigerator over night or for at least 8 hours.
- Place the prawns on skewers – six to a skewer and two skewers for a serving.
- Coat with any remaining marinade and barbecue, grill or broil until cooked, turning halfway.

Balsamic Black Garlic and Halibut

Ingredients (Serves 2)

- 2 Halibut Steaks

- 2 tablespoons of Balsamic Vinegar
- 2 finely sliced cloves of Black Garlic
- Juice of 1 small Lemon
- 1 teaspoon of Lemon Zest
- 1 teaspoon of Olive Oil or Rapeseed Oil
- Freshly ground Black Pepper, Sea Salt and a little Sweetener to taste
- Fresh Coriander (Cilantro) to garnish

Method

- Mix the balsamic vinegar, lemon juice and lemon zest in a bowl and add sweetener and salt and pepper to taste.
- Heat the oil in a pan over medium-high heat and add the black garlic.

- Dip both sides of the halibut steak in the balsamic mixture and cook in the pan for approximately 5 minutes each side. The fish is cooked when you can flake the fish with a fork.
- Serve immediately garnished with a little coriander.

Tomato Tuna Soufflé

Ingredients (Serves 2)

- A tin of very well drained tuna flakes – in spring water or brine depending on whether you are watching your salt intake
- 2 teaspoons of tomato paste/purée
- 4 finely sliced scallions/ spring onions
- 4 whole eggs

- 3 rounded tablespoons of fat free fromage frais or fat free ricotta cheese
- 1 teaspoon of olive oil/rapeseed oil to grease dishes

Method

- Separate the eggs and putting the egg whites into a large bowl and the yolks into another large bowl.
- Whisk the egg whites until stiff
- Put the tomato paste/ puree, fromage frais or ricotta cheese and scallions/ spring onions into the bowl with the egg yolk and mix well.
- Stir in the well drained tuna flakes.

- Then fold the egg white slowly into this mixture taking care to keep as much air in the mixture as possible.
- Pour into oiled souffle dish or dishes
- Bake in a preheated oven for about 35 to 40 minutes at 150 ° C , 300°F or Gas Mark 2. Using small dishes will reduce the cooking time needed.

Stuffed Grilled Calamari

Ingredients (Serves 8 as a starter or 4 as a main course)

- 8 squid bodies rinsed and halved crosswise
- 4 medium ripe tomatoes, seeded and diced
- 1 head of chopped frisee/curly endive/chicory

- 1/3 of a cucumber cut into matchsticks
- 4 finely sliced scallions/spring onions
- 4 teaspoon extra-virgin olive oil
- 1 lemon, zested and juiced
- Sea salt and freshly ground black pepper

Method

- Heat a stove-top griddle or get your barbecue started and up to cooking temperature.
- In a small bowl make a simple salad dressing using the lemon juice, lemon zest, 3 teaspoons of olive oil and salt and pepper.
- In a large bowl toss the tomatoes, frisee, cucumber and scallions/spring onions.
- Drizzle the dressing over the salad stuffing.

- Put about a tablespoon of the stuffing into each squid.
- Brush with the remaining teaspoon of olive oil.
- Grill for 4 to 5 minutes on a high heat turning frequently. Don't over cook or the squid can become tough.
- Lemon Zesty Grilled Calamari with Garlic
- Ingredients (Serves 4)

- 4 Squid (weighing about 225g or 8oz each) cleaned, rinsed and dried with kitchen paper
- The juice and zest of one lemon and one lemon cut into quarters to garnish
- Sea Salt and freshly ground Black Pepper
- 2 teaspoons of Olive Oil
- 2 finely diced cloves of Garlic

- Fresh chopped Coriander/Cilantro/coriander to garnish

Method

- ❖ Cut the squid open by slicing down the side of the tube.
- ❖ Carefully score the inside of the flesh in a diamond pattern making sure not to cut all the way through.
- ❖ In a bowl mix the lemon juice, lemon zest, garlic,olive oil and salt and pepper.
- ❖ Rub the marinade into the squid, cover the bowl with cling film and leave to marinate for at least two hours in the refrigerator.
- ❖ Heat your barbecue or griddle until hot
- ❖ Place the squid on the heat for about two minutes each side.

- ❖ Serve on a plate garnished with the fresh chopped cilantro/coriander and a lemon quarter
- ❖ Squeeze the lemon juice on the squid just before eating.

Summer Squid Salad

Ingredients(Serves 4)

- ❖ 1 and 1/2 pounds of Squid Rings, about 3/4″ wide
- ❖ Juice of one Lemon
- ❖ 4 teaspoons of extra-virgin Olive Oil
- ❖ 1 pinch of Cayenne Pepper
- ❖ Sea Salt and freshly ground Black Pepper
- ❖ 3 to 4 finely chopped and seeded Tomatoes
  - o finely chopped Red Onion
  - o tablespoons of Capers

- tablespoons of chopped fresh Cilantro/Coriander

Method

- Steam the squid rings over simmering water for 3 to 4 minutes.
- Remove the squid and immediately immerse the squid in iced water to stop the cooking process.
- When cold take out of the water and drain thoroughly.
- About one or two hours before serving whisk the lemon juice, olive oil, salt, black pepper and cayenne pepper together in a large bowl.
- Add the squid, tomatoes, onion, capers and cilantro/coriander and mix together.

- Cover and refrigerate for 1 hour before serving on a bed of mixed lettuce leaves.

Calamari Tomato and Fennel Stew

Ingredients (Serves 4)

- 2 pounds of Calamari Rings
  - chopped Fennel Bulb
  - sliced Red Onions
- 500 g of fresh peeled Cherry Tomatoes
  - x 400g (14 oz) cans of Crushed/Chopped Tomatoes
- 250ml or 1 cup of Chicken Stock
  - teaspoons of Olive Oil
- 3 tablespoons of chopped Parsley
- 1 tablespoon of Paprika
  - chopped cloves of Garlic
- Sea Salt and freshly ground Black Pepper

Method

- o Fry the onion and fennel in a large pan over a medium-high heat for about 5 minutes and they start to brown
- o Add the garlic, chicken stock and tinned tomatoes and mix together.
- o Increase the heat to high and continue stirring until the volume is reduced by half.
- o Add the fresh peeled tomatoes and reduce the heat to a gentle simmer.
- o Stir in the calamari and simmer for at least 1 hour and keep cooking until the calamari is tender.
- o Season to taste with salt and pepper and then stir in the chopped parsley and serve.

Herby Halibut and Vegetable Kebabs

Ingredients (Serves 4)

- and 1/2 pounds halibut, cut into 1″ to 1 1/2″ chunks
- tablespoons of fresh finely chopped herbs of your choice such as basil, thyme, sage, marjoram or rosemary
- zucchini/courgettes cut into 16 1/2″ slices
- 16 mini plum tomatoes or large cherry tomatoes
- 2 bell peppers cut into 16 "squares"
- 2 small red onion cut into 16 pieces
  - teaspoons extra-virgin olive oil,
- 3 tablespoons fresh lemon juice
- 2 finely diced garlic cloves

Method

- Put 1 tablespoon of the fresh mixed herbs in a large bowl with 2 teaspoons of olive oil and 1 tablespoon of lemon juice and mix together.
- Add the vegetables and toss in the mixture to coat.
- Thread your vegetables onto the skewers and then cover and place in the refrigerator for up to 4 hours.
- Add 2 teaspoons of oil and 2 tablespoon of lemon juice to the bowl and stir together with the remaining fresh herbs and the garlic.
- Add the fish chunks and stir to coat.
- Cover and refrigerate for between 1 and 2 hours.

- Thread the fish chunks onto 4 skewers and season with a little sea salt and freshly ground black pepper.
- The vegetable kebabs will take a couple of minutes longer to cook than the halibut so place these on your barbecue first.
- After a couple of minutes add your fish kebabs and continue to cook both for between 8 and 10 minutes until the fish is cooked.
- Don't forget to turn your kebabs and use any remaining marinade to coat during the cooking.

Dukan Diet Recipe: Plank Salmon

I decided to keep the barbecue theme going for this post too, making it three barbecue recipes in a row. This recipe can be used on any day of the Dukan Diet except Dukan Thursdays in Stabilisation.

I must admit than when I was quite a lot younger than I am now, I thought that Plank Salmon was a type of salmon rather than salmon cooked on a plank! The most popular planks to cook on are made from cedar wood which adds a mild smoky taste that is sweet and spicy but you can also get planks made form other woods such as alder or maple.

Although you can use planks to cook lots of different foods they are perfect for cooking fish on the barbecue. The plank means you don't have to worry about your fish falling apart or sticking to the grill and you end up with a piece of fish that is juicier and more full of flavor. Using a plank also means that you need less oil.

If you have not used a plank to cook with before you may find the information in this link useful.

Plank Salmon

Ingredients (Serves 4)

- 4 x 6 oz salmon fillets
- 4 teaspoons of extra virgin olive oil
  - finely diced large red onion

o sliced lemons

o Freshly ground black pepper

Method

o Soak your cedar plank as directed or for approximately 12 hours. Weight the plank down with a brick or other heavy object to keep it submerged.

o Preheat your barbecue to high heat.

o Place your prepared plank on the grill and grill for 2 to 3 minutes until dry and then reduce heat to a medium heat.

o While waiting for your plank to dry rub the salmon fillets with olive oil.

o Place the fillets on the dry plank and top with the finely diced red onion, lots of freshly ground black pepper and lemon slices.

o Place the plank on the cooler side of the grill and cook until salmon is easily flaked with a fork.

Shrimp and Spinach Oriental Salad

Ingredients (Serves 4)

o 600g of cooked peeled shrimps (prawns)
o 300g of fresh spinach
    o thinly sliced red bell pepper
o 1 large grated carrot
o 1 large finely diced onion
    o cloves of finely diced garlic
    o tablespoons of white vinegar
o 1 tablespoon of tomato puree
o 2 tablespoon of soy sauce

- 1 tablespoon of finely grated fresh ginger
  - teaspoons of rapeseed oil
- Sweetener, sea salt and freshly ground black pepper to taste

Method

- Put the onion, garlic, vinegar, tomato puree, soy sauce, ginger and rapeseed oil into a food processor and blend until combined.
- Place in a large bowl and add the sweetener, salt and pepper to taste.
- Add the remaining ingredients and toss until evenly coated and serve!

Salmon in "Wasabi" Sauce

Ingredients (Serves 4)

- 4 pieces of salmon fillet
- 4 teaspoons of rapeseed oil
- 4 scallions/spring onions
- 2 cloves of garlic
    - small bunch of fresh cilantro/coriander
- 4 tablespoons of fat free Greek yogurt
- 6 tablespoons of lemon juice sweetened to taste with sweetener
- Salt and pepper to taste
- 1 tablespoon of "wasabi" paste

Method

- Peel and finely chop the garlic.

- Wash and chop the cilantro/coriander, keeping back a few leaves to garnish the finished dish
- Wash the scallions/spring onions and finely slice.
- Season the fish with salt and pepper
- Heat oil in a non-stick pan and fry the salmon at a medium heat on each side for approximately 5 minutes.
- Mix the yogurt in a bowl with two tablespoon of sweetened lemon juice until smooth .
- Add garlic and spring onions to the salmon and sauté for 2 minutes.
- Remove the salmon from the pan and keep warm on a serving dish
- Add the remaining sweetened lemon juice and allow to cool slightly before stirring in the yogurt.

- Add the wasabi paste and allow to dissolve in the sauce before stirring in the chopped cilantro/coriander.
- Pour the sauce over the salmon fillets and garnish before serving.

Baked Zucchini Chips or Courgette Crisps

Ingredients

- large zucchini or courgette
- 1 teaspoon of olive oil
- Sea salt or other seasoning of your choice

Method

- Preheat oven to 225°Fahrenheit, 110° Celsius or Gas mark 1/4.
- Thinly slice the zucchini/courgette crossways into medallions or length ways into strips if the zucchini/courgette is not very big.
- Brush olive oil thinly onto a small piece of foil and use this to oil one side on each zucchini/courgette by placing on the foil
- Replace oil on the foil as needed.
- Place your slices on a silicone baking sheet oil side up and sprinkle sparingly with your seasoning.
- Place in preheated oven and bake 45 minutes.
- Turn the baking sheet to ensure even cooking and continue baking until done to your liking.

- Allow to cool and enjoy as soon as possible!!
- Carrot and Zucchini (Courgette) Soup

Ingredients

  - finely diced medium onion
- 1lb of peeled and sliced carrots
- 1lb of sliced unpeeled zucchini/courgettes
  - teaspoons of curry powder
  - 1/2 cups of chicken or vegetable stock
- Handful of freshly chopped parsley
- Sprigs of parsley to garnish.

Method

- Dry fry the onions in pan until soft adding a little stock as needed.

- Add carrots, zucchini (courgettes),curry powder and the remainder of the stock.
- Bring to the boil and then reduce the heat to allow the vegetables to simmer for 20 minutes tender.
- Add the chopped parsley.
- Blend the soup until smooth using a hand blender or liquidizer.
- Garnish with a sprig of parsley to serve

Main Course

The Roast Turkey is of course a must have but you need to ensure that your serving is breast meat with all skin removed and if you do cook roast potatoes for your guests you will need to keep them off your plate!!

Stuffing Patties

Make your own stuffing using a mixture of oat bran, celery, mushrooms, onions, egg, low fat bacon and minced lean pork but rather than stuffing the turkey place equal amounts of the stuffing in a non stick muffin tray.

Vegetables

Cauliflower Mash – You will find three recipes for different versions of this vegetable, Baked Mashed Cauliflower, Garlicky Cauliflower Mash and Parsnip and Cauliflower Mash Up in my post Dukan Diet Cruise Phase Recipes – Cauliflower Mash

Carrot and Butternut Squash Puree

Ingredients

- o pound of peeled and sliced carrots
- 1 pound of peeled and cubed butternut squash
- 1/8 teaspoon of nutmeg
- Freshly ground black pepper

Method

- Steam carrots and squash until tender.
- Transfer to food processor and add nutmeg.
- Blend until smooth.
- Season with freshly ground pepper if desired before transferring to serving dish.

Sautéed Green Beans

Ingredients

- o 1/2 pounds green beans, trimmed
- 1 tablespoon of finely diced shallots
- 1 clove of finely diced garlic
- Freshly ground black pepper
- Lemon zest

Method

- ❖ Simmer green beans for 4-5 minutes.
- ❖ Remove from heat, and drain the beans.
- ❖ Plunge them into ice-cold water to halt the cooking process and retain their color.
- ❖ Dry fry the garlic and shallots in a little water if needed.

❖ After three minutes add the beans and continue cooking for a further three minutes.

❖ Season with pepper and stir in lemon zest just before serving.

Dessert

Pumpkin Pie Custard Recipe (serves 10)

Ingredients

❖ 2 cups of canned pumpkin

❖ 8 egg whites

  o can of fat-free evaporated milk (This is not a permitted ingredient and adds around 300 calories to the whole recipe but this is only 30 calories a serving and as Thanksgiving only comes around once a year I think it is

a treat that can be fitted in for the
difference it makes to the taste!)

* 1/2 cup skim milk
* Sweetener – equivalent to about 3/4 cup of
  sugar
* 1/4 teaspoon of salt
* 1/4 teaspoon of ground cloves
* 1/4 teaspoon of ground nutmeg
* 1 teaspoon of ground cinnamon
* 1/2 teaspoon of ground ginger

Method

* In a large bowl, beat the pumpkin, egg
  whites, evaporated milk and skim milk until
  smooth.
* Add the sweetener and salt and spices,
  mixing well.

- ❖ Spoon into ten 6-oz. ramekins coated with low fat cooking spray.
- ❖ Cook in oven preheated to 350°F, 175°C or Gas Mark 4 until a knife inserted near the center comes out clean, this should be approximately 40 to 45 minutes.
- ❖ Allow to cool before placing in the refrigerator.
- ❖ Remove from refrigerator just before serving and top with a little sweetened fat free Greek yogurt if desired and a sprig of mint.

Lumpy Dukan Miracle Soup

Ingredients (5 or 6 servings)

- ❖ Half a head of cabbage
- ❖ 2 large onions

- ❖ 5 or 6 spring onions (scallions) for garnish
- ❖ 2 tins of chopped tomatoes
- ❖ 3 carrots
- ❖ A head of celery
- ❖ 2 green peppers (bell peppers)
- ❖ 3 chicken bouillon/stock cubes (Vegetarians should use vegetable bouillon/stock cubes
- ❖ Seasoning of choice such as herbs, curry powder or freshly ground black pepper

Method

- ❖ Prepare all vegetables and cut all except the spring onions in large bite size pieces.
- ❖ Finely slice the spring onions and reserve to garnish.
- ❖ Place all the other ingredient in a stockpot or large saucepan and cover with water.

- ❖ Bring to the boil and cook for ten minutes.
- ❖ Reduce the heat and simmer until all vegetables are cooked and tender.

Roasted Red Pepper and Carrot Soup

Ingredients

- ❖ 2 large red bell peppers
  - ○ teaspoon of olive oil (new addition now allowed on the Dukan Diet)
- ❖ 1/2 teaspoon of curry powder
- ❖ 1 bay leaf
- ❖ 1 large sliced onion
  - ○ large sliced carrots
  - ○ cloves of peeled and diced garlic
- ❖ Sea salt and freshly ground black pepper to taste

Method

❖ Preheat oven to 350°F, 180°C or Gas Mark 4.

❖ Place bell peppers on baking sheet and roast for about 1 hour turning occasionally. The skin should be wrinkled and blackened all over.

❖ Put the peppers in a plastic bag and when cool rub off the skin and remove any seeds.

❖ Heat the oil in pan over medium heat

❖ Add the curry powder and bay leaf and stir 10 seconds.

❖ Then add the onion, carrots and garlic

❖ If you want to omit the oil, dry fry the onions first in a little water then add the bay leaf and curry powder before adding the carrots and garlic.

❖ Cover until onion is soft.

❖ Add 4 cups of water and the cooked peppers and bring to the boil.

❖ Reduce heat to simmer continue cooking for a further 30 minutes.

❖ Transfer the mixture to a liquidizer or use a hand blender and puree until smooth.

❖ Season to taste and serve.

Carrot and Zucchini (Courgette) Soup

Ingredients

o finely diced medium onion

❖ 1lb of peeled and sliced carrots

❖ 1lb of sliced unpeeled zucchini/courgettes

o teaspoons of curry powder

- 1/2 cups of chicken or vegetable stock
- ❖ Handful of freshly chopped parsley
- ❖ Sprigs of parsley to garnish.

Method

- ❖ Dry fry the onions in pan until soft adding a little stock as needed.
- ❖ Add carrots, zucchini (courgettes),curry powder and the remainder of the stock.
- ❖ Bring to the boil and then reduce the heat to allow the vegetables to simmer for 20 minutes tender.
- ❖ Add the chopped parsley.
- ❖ Blend the soup until smooth using a hand blender or liquidizer.
- ❖ Garnish with a sprig of parsley to serve

Main Course

The Roast Turkey is of course a must have but you need to ensure that your serving is breast meat with all skin removed and if you do cook roast potatoes for your guests you will need to keep them off your plate!!

Stuffing Patties

Make your own stuffing using a mixture of oat bran, celery, mushrooms, onions, egg, low fat bacon and minced lean pork but rather than stuffing the turkey place equal amounts of the stuffing in a non stick muffin tray.

Vegetables

Cauliflower Mash – You will find three recipes for different versions of this vegetable, Baked Mashed Cauliflower, Garlicky Cauliflower Mash and Parsnip and Cauliflower Mash Up in my post Dukan Diet Cruise Phase Recipes – Cauliflower Mash

Carrot and Butternut Squash Puree

Ingredients

1 pound of peeled and sliced carrots

1 pound of peeled and cubed butternut squash

❖ 1/8 teaspoon of nutmeg

Freshly ground black pepper

Method

- ❖ Steam carrots and squash until tender.
- ❖ Transfer to food processor and add nutmeg.
- ❖ Blend until smooth.
- ❖ Season with freshly ground pepper if desired before transferring to serving dish.

Sautéed Green Beans

Ingredients

- o 1/2 pounds green beans, trimmed
- ❖ 1 tablespoon of finely diced shallots
- ❖ 1 clove of finely diced garlic
- ❖ Freshly ground black pepper
- ❖ Lemon zest

Method

- ❖ Simmer green beans for 4-5 minutes.
- ❖ Remove from heat, and drain the beans.
- ❖ Plunge them into ice-cold water to halt the cooking process and retain their color.
- ❖ Dry fry the garlic and shallots in a little water if needed.
- ❖ After three minutes add the beans and continue cooking for a further three minutes.
- ❖ Season with pepper and stir in lemon zest just before serving.

Dessert

Pumpkin Pie Custard Recipe (serves 10)

Ingredients

- ❖ 2 cups of canned pumpkin
- ❖ 8 egg whites
  - ○ can of fat-free evaporated milk (This is not a permitted ingredient and adds around 300 calories to the whole recipe but this is only 30 calories a serving and as Thanksgiving only comes around once a year I think it is a treat that can be fitted in for the difference it makes to the taste!)
- ❖ 1/2 cup skim milk
- ❖ Sweetener – equivalent to about 3/4 cup of sugar
- ❖ 1/4 teaspoon of salt
- ❖ 1/4 teaspoon of ground cloves
- ❖ 1/4 teaspoon of ground nutmeg
- ❖ 1 teaspoon of ground cinnamon
- ❖ 1/2 teaspoon of ground ginger

Method

❖ In a large bowl, beat the pumpkin, egg whites, evaporated milk and skim milk until smooth.

❖ Add the sweetener and salt and spices, mixing well.

❖ Spoon into ten 6-oz. ramekins coated with low fat cooking spray.

❖ Cook in oven preheated to 350°F, 175°C or Gas Mark 4 until a knife inserted near the center comes out clean, this should be approximately 40 to 45 minutes.

❖ Allow to cool before placing in the refrigerator.

❖ Remove from refrigerator just before serving and top with a little sweetened fat free Greek yogurt if desired and a sprig of mint.

Carrot and Zucchini (Courgette) Soup

Ingredients

- o finely diced medium onion
- ➢ 1lb of peeled and sliced carrots
- ➢ 1lb of sliced unpeeled zucchini/courgettes
  - o teaspoons of curry powder
  - o 1/2 cups of chicken or vegetable stock
- ➢ Handful of freshly chopped parsley
- ➢ Sprigs of parsley to garnish.

Method

- Dry fry the onions in pan until soft adding a little stock as needed.
- Add carrots, zucchini (courgettes),curry powder and the remainder of the stock.
- Bring to the boil and then reduce the heat to allow the vegetables to simmer for 20 minutes tender.
- Add the chopped parsley.
- Blend the soup until smooth using a hand blender or liquidizer.
- Garnish with a sprig of parsley to serve

Main Course

The Roast Turkey is of course a must have but you need to ensure that your serving is breast meat with all skin removed and if you do cook roast potatoes for your guests you will need to keep them off your plate!!

Stuffing Patties

Make your own stuffing using a mixture of oat bran, celery, mushrooms, onions, egg, low fat bacon and minced lean pork but rather than stuffing the turkey place equal amounts of the stuffing in a non stick muffin tray.

Vegetables

Cauliflower Mash – You will find three recipes for different versions of this vegetable, Baked Mashed Cauliflower, Garlicky Cauliflower Mash and Parsnip and Cauliflower Mash Up in my post Dukan Diet Cruise Phase Recipes – Cauliflower Mash

Carrot and Butternut Squash Puree

Ingredients

- o pound of peeled and sliced carrots
- ➤ 1 pound of peeled and cubed butternut squash
- ➤ 1/8 teaspoon of nutmeg
- ➤ Freshly ground black pepper

Method

- ➤ Steam carrots and squash until tender.
- ➤ Transfer to food processor and add nutmeg.
- ➤ Blend until smooth.

- ➢ Season with freshly ground pepper if desired before transferring to serving dish.

Sautéed Green Beans

Ingredients

- o 1/2 pounds green beans, trimmed
- ➢ 1 tablespoon of finely diced shallots
- ➢ 1 clove of finely diced garlic
- ➢ Freshly ground black pepper
- ➢ Lemon zest

Method

- ➢ Simmer green beans for 4-5 minutes.
- ➢ Remove from heat, and drain the beans.

- Plunge them into ice-cold water to halt the cooking process and retain their color.
- Dry fry the garlic and shallots in a little water if needed.
- After three minutes add the beans and continue cooking for a further three minutes.
- Season with pepper and stir in lemon zest just before serving.

Dessert

Pumpkin Pie Custard Recipe (serves 10)

Ingredients

- 2 cups of canned pumpkin
- 8 egg whites
  - can of fat-free evaporated milk (This is not a permitted ingredient and adds

around 300 calories to the whole recipe but this is only 30 calories a serving and as Thanksgiving only comes around once a year I think it is a treat that can be fitted in for the difference it makes to the taste!)

- 1/2 cup skim milk
- Sweetener – equivalent to about 3/4 cup of sugar
- 1/4 teaspoon of salt
- 1/4 teaspoon of ground cloves
- 1/4 teaspoon of ground nutmeg
- 1 teaspoon of ground cinnamon
- 1/2 teaspoon of ground ginger

Method

➤ In a large bowl, beat the pumpkin, egg whites, evaporated milk and skim milk until smooth.

➤ Add the sweetener and salt and spices, mixing well.

➤ Spoon into ten 6-oz. ramekins coated with low fat cooking spray.

➤ Cook in oven preheated to 350°F, 175°C or Gas Mark 4 until a knife inserted near the center comes out clean, this should be approximately 40 to 45 minutes.

➤ Allow to cool before placing in the refrigerator.

➤ Remove from refrigerator just before serving and top with a little sweetened fat free Greek yogurt if desired and a sprig of mint.

Dukan Diet Cruise Phase Recipes – Cauliflower Rice

Making Cauliflower Rice couldn't be simpler, just watch the video below and see how easy it is. After you've watched the video you can think about how you are going to use Cauliflower Rice on your PV days in the Cruise Phase of the Dukan Diet. To help you along I've included my recipe for Indian Cauliflower Rice after the video.

The video uses fresh cauliflower but you can also use frozen. Just microwave it for around three minutes to soften it a little, then shred in your food processor. Put the cauliflower in your microwaveable bowl, cover and microwave for another three or four minutes to finish.

Indian Cauliflower Rice

Ingredients

1 medium cauliflower

1 medium onion

1 teaspoon fennel seeds

2 teaspoons turmeric

1 teaspoon paprika

1 teaspoon cumin

Method

Rice your cauliflower in the food processor.

Chop the onion and dry fry with the spices until soft, adding a little water if needed.

Add the cauliflower and continue cooking until done. Again you can add a little water but don't over do the water and don't over cook.

Dukan Pizza Base

Ingredients

2 cups of cold cooked cauliflower rice

1 egg and 1 egg white

1 tablespoon of oat bran

2 Light Babybels

Salt and pepper

Method

Finely shred or grate cheese into a bowl.

Add the cauliflower and oat bran and mix well.

Add the eggs and seasoning and combine into a dough.

Spread thinly onto a silicone baking sheet or a baking sheet sprayed with a little oil.

Bake in a hot oven until the pizza crust looks crunchy around the edges. This will probably be around 15 minutes but it will depend on how thick or thin you've made your base.

You are now ready to add the toppings to your pizza. I use a little tomato puree and whatever vegetables I have to hand thinly sliced. I then finish with another couple of shredded light Babybels and sprinkle with some fresh herbs.

Return your pizza to the oven to cook the topping for another 10 to 15 minutes.

Baked Mashed Cauliflower

Ingredients

1 medium to large cauliflower

Zero fat yogurt as needed

Salt & pepper

Paprika

Method

Break the cauliflower in to florets and steam until tender.

Put the cauliflower and the salt and pepper in blender and blitz until smooth, adding a little yogurt as needed to give the consistency preferred.

Pour the mixture into an oven proof dish and sprinkle with paprika.

Bake in a hot oven until the top has browned slightly.

Garlicky Cauliflower Mash

Ingredients

1 medium cauliflower

3 tablespoons of zero fat Greek yogurt.

1 teaspoon minced garlic

Salt and freshly ground black pepper

1 teaspoon chopped fresh chives, for garnish

Method

Break the cauliflower in to florets and steam until just tender.

Put the cauliflower, garlic, yogurt and salt and pepper in blender and blitz trying to leave a little texture in the mixture.

Serve garnished with the chopped chives.

Parsnip and Cauliflower Mash Up

Ingredients

1 small cauliflower broken into florets

450 grams of peeled and chopped parsnips

2 cloves of minced garlic

salt and pepper

4 tablespoons of zero fat creme fraiche

Method

Steam the cauliflower and parsnips until tender.

Place the cauliflower and parsnip in blender with a little salt and pepper and the minced garlic and blitz until smooth.

Add the creme fraiche and blitz again and more salt and pepper if needed.

Conclusion

Dissimilar to other high-protein diets, this plan focuses on lean protein sources over those high in saturated fat. Furthermore, protein can make you feel fuller longer, helping you shed pounds.

The downside is that this plan doesn't teach deep rooted healthy eating propensities. Even more problematic, it recommends that you stay in the consolidation phase until you reach your goal. In the event that you have a lot of weight to lose, this stage could go on for quite a long time or even years, which could lead to a healthfully inadequate diet.

On the off chance that you're looking to lose a relatively small measure of weight fast, this diet may work for you. On the off chance that you are more than 50 or have a condition, like diabetes, or need to lose a lot of weight, talk to your PCP first.